Seasons of the Year

Spring

by Karen Bischer

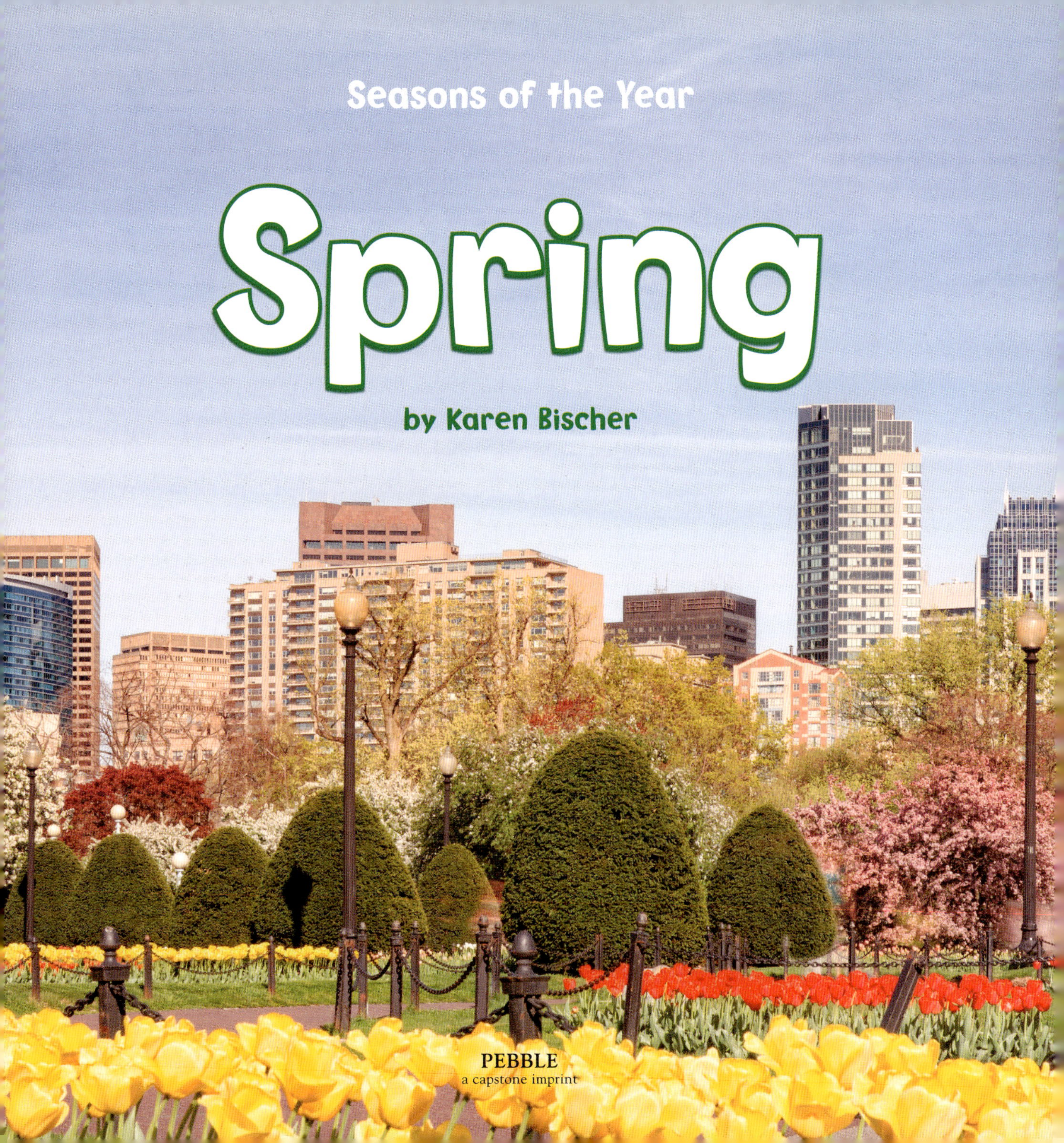

PEBBLE
a capstone imprint

Published by Pebble, an imprint of Capstone
1710 Roe Crest Drive, North Mankato, Minnesota 56003
capstonepub.com

Copyright © 2025 by Capstone. All rights reserved. No part of this publication may be reproduced in whole or in part, or stored in a retrieval system, or transmitted in any form or by any means, electronic, mechanical, photocopying, recording, or otherwise, without written permission of the publisher.

Library of Congress Cataloging-in-Publication Data is available on the Library of Congress website.
ISBN: 9780756591120 (hardcover)
ISBN: 9780756591175 (paperback)
ISBN: 9780756591168 (ebook PDF)

Summary: Spring has sprung! Farmers are planting their fields. Birds are building their nests. People are out for walks in the warmer temperatures. Discover the many ways spring affects weather, plants, animals, people, and more.

Editorial Credits
Editor: Christopher Harbo; Designer: Sarah Bennett; Media Researcher: Svetlana Zhurkin; Production Specialist: Katy LaVigne

Image Credits
Getty Images: Ariel Skelley, 17, fotokostic, 13, SolStock, 5; Shutterstock: Agnieszka Gaul, 1, Alexsander Ovsyannikov, 10, Ami Parikh, 18, DFLC Prints, 9, Evgeniy_16, 14, grayjay, 6, 7, Ms Moloko (background), cover and throughout, Mykola Mazuryk, 11, NCAimages, 12, Noppasin Wongchum, 8, S Curtis, 4, Shawn.ccf, 19, Sophon Nawit, 20, Stuart Monk, 16, Tatyana Tomsickova, cover (top), Tony Campbell, 15, Valenty, cover (bottom left), 23

Any additional websites and resources referenced in this book are not maintained, authorized, or sponsored by Capstone. All product and company names are trademarks™ or registered® trademarks of their respective holders.

Table of Contents

It's Spring!... 4
Days Get Longer 6
Spring Here, Fall There 8
Spring Weather... 10
Plants in Spring 12
Animals in Spring 14
People in Spring 16
Spring Is a Wonderful Thing!............... 18

    Be a Bird Watcher!.......................... 20
    Glossary... 22
    Read More.. 23
    Internet Sites 23
    Index.. 24
    About the Author........................... 24

Words in **bold** are in the glossary.

It's Spring!

Winter's cold grip is easing up. Days are getting longer. Birds and animals are on the move. Some are having babies! Warm weather has returned. People are growing gardens and playing outside. Spring is in full swing!

Days Get Longer

Earth has two **hemispheres**, or halves. At the start of spring in the northern hemisphere, the sun's light shines equally on both halves. As the season goes on, Earth's **tilt** causes the northern half to get more and more sunlight over time. Days become longer. Nights become shorter.

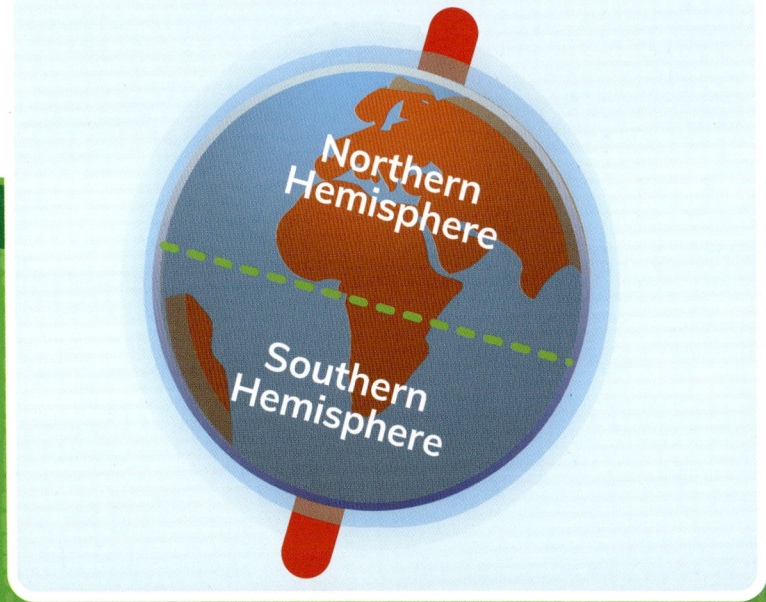

The Seasons

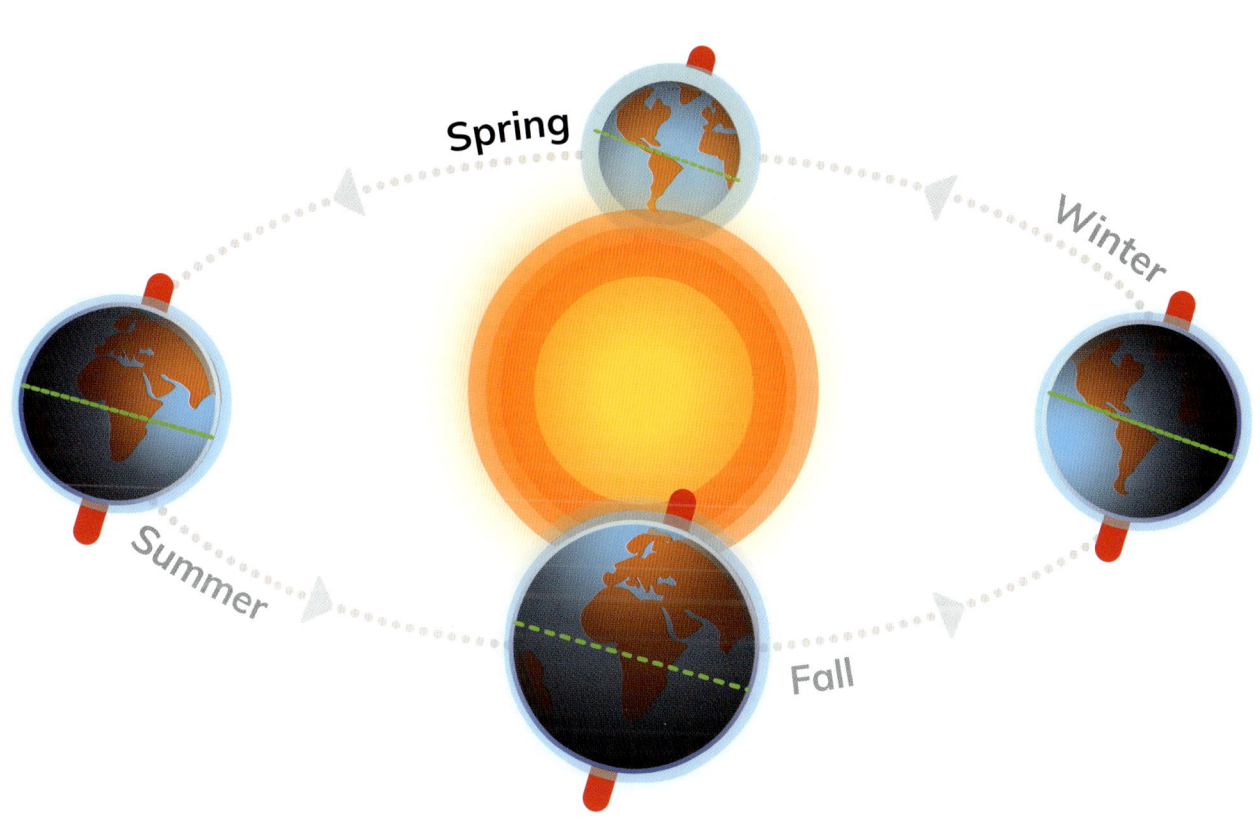

Spring Here, Fall There

Earth's hemispheres have opposite seasons. The northern hemisphere has spring from late March through late June. At that same time, fall happens in the southern hemisphere. While you have spring, people in the other hemisphere have fall.

Trees showing fall colors in Chile in May

Spring Weather

Spring has a wide range of weather. Days start getting warmer. Snow and ice melt. Some places have dry and sunny weather. Others are foggy and rainy. Most **tornadoes** happen in spring. Many rainbows happen this time of year too!

Plants in Spring

Spring sunshine and rain help plants grow. The grass turns green. Bare trees **sprout** new leaves. Flowers start to **bloom**.

In spring, farmers also plant seeds in their fields. These seeds sprout and grow into **crops**.

Animals in Spring

Animals are on the move in spring! **Hibernation** ends. Bears and hedgehogs wake up between March and May. Many birds **migrate** north as well.

In spring, many animals have babies. Birds build nests and lay eggs. Deer, foxes, and squirrels raise their young.

People in Spring

Warm spring weather gets people outside! They plant gardens and mow the lawn. Kids play baseball, softball, and tennis outdoors. Families go hiking, biking, and have picnics on sunny days. People also celebrate Earth Day in spring.

Spring Is a Wonderful Thing!

Spring is a season of growth. The days have more sunlight. The air feels warmer. Animals wake up from long winter naps.

What do you like best about spring? Is it blooming flowers or having picnics? It's hard to choose. Spring is a wonderful thing!

Be a Bird Watcher!

There may be more types of birds in your area than you think. How many can you find?

What You Need
- binoculars
- cellphone
- notebook
- colored pencils
- pencil

What You Do

1. Pick a spot in your yard or visit a local park with an adult.

2. Use binoculars to look for different types of birds. Birds migrate in spring, so you may see many kinds.

3. Use a cellphone to take a picture of each type of bird you see.

4. Draw each bird you photograph in a notebook using colored pencils. Next to each bird, write the date and place you saw it.

5. Use a website or library book about birds to look up the birds you drew. Write the name of each bird you can identify next to its drawing.

6. During the year, keep looking for birds in the same spot. Which birds show up all year? Which ones come and go?

Glossary

bloom (BLOOM)—to flower

crop (KROP)—a plant farmers grow in large amounts, usually for food

hemisphere (HEM-uhss-fihr)—one half of Earth; the equator divides Earth into northern and southern hemispheres

hibernation (hye-bur-NAY-shuhn)—a long winter sleep of some animals in cold climates

migrate (MYE-grate)—to move from one place to another

sprout (SPROWT)—to start to grow

tilt (TILT)—an angle or lean; not straight

tornado (tor-NAY-doh)—a spinning column of air that looks like a funnel and can destroy anything in its path

Read More

Carr, Aaron, and Heather Kissock. *Spring*. New York: Lightbox Learning, Inc., 2024.

Press, J. P. *Spring Plants*. Minneapolis: Bearport Publishing, 2022.

Schell, Lily. *Spring*. Minneapolis: Bellwether Media, 2023.

Internet Sites

Arbor Day Foundation: Photosynthesis
arborday.org/kids/photosynthesis

Britannica Kids: Spring
kids.britannica.com/kids/article/spring/623337

Cornell Lab: All About Birds
allaboutbirds.org

Index

animals, 4, 14, 18

days, 4, 6, 10, 16, 18

Earth, 6, 8, 16

flowers, 12, 18

hemispheres, 6, 8

hibernation, 14

migration, 14

nights, 6

people, 4, 8, 16

plants, 12, 18

rainbows, 10

tornadoes, 10

trees, 9, 12

weather, 4, 10, 16, 18

About the Author

Karen Bischer is a writer and New Jersey resident who loves watching sports, especially baseball. When she's not cheering on her beloved New York Yankees, you can find her playing with (or being bossed around by) her cat, Clarence, and dog, Brandy.